Holiday Appetizers

Publications International, Ltd.
Favorite Brand Name Recipes at www.fbnr.com

Microwave Cooking: Microwave ovens vary in wattage. Use the cooking times as guidelines and check for doneness before adding more time.

Preparation/Cooking Times: Preparation times are based on the approximate amount of time required to assemble the recipe before cooking, baking, chilling or serving. These times include preparation steps such as measuring, chopping and mixing. The fact that some preparations and cooking can be done simultaneously is taken into account. Preparation of optional ingredients and serving suggestions is not included.

contents

introduction

If your holiday wish this year is for more time, you've come to the right place! As you read through the pages of *Holiday Appetizers,* look for recipes with the "make-ahead" icon. This icon is your indication that a portion or all of the recipe can be prepared ahead of the party.

make-ahead	recipe

To save even more time, follow these helpful tips.

★ Always follow the recipe instructions for maximum food storage time.

★ To reduce the risk of harmful bacteria growth, quickly cool hot food in the refrigerator before freezing. When the food is cool to the touch, place it in the freezer.

★ To avoid freezer burn, always store food in tightly sealed containers. If you are using resealable freezer bags, be sure to press out any excess air.

★ Cheeses, dips and spreads quickly absorb odors from other foods being stored in the refrigerator. Keep them in airtight containers or in tightly sealed plastic storage bags.

★ The safest and best method for defrosting frozen food is thawing it in the refrigerator.

★ Never refreeze food that has been frozen and thawed. The flavor is adversely affected and the chance for bacteria growth increases greatly.

★ When freezing food, label containers with the date the food should be consumed by or with the date it was placed in the freezer.

Why not try this exciting make-ahead menu for your next holiday party?

Start the party off with the **Cranberry-Orange Snack Mix** (page 48) or **Citrus Candied Nuts** (page 53). Both recipes can be prepared up to two weeks before the event. Be sure to follow the recipe directions for proper storage.

The **Pesto Cheese Wreath** (page 26) can be prepared the night before the party. Serve this delicious spread with an assortment of crackers or fresh vegetables, such as broccoli florets, baby carrots or celery sticks.

Next bring out the **Louisiana Crab Dip with Crudités** (page 24) and **Venezuelan Salsa** (page 54). Prepare these easy-to- make appetizers the morning of the party. Refrigerate them until you are ready to serve. (If you are cutting the crudités up ahead of time, refrigerate them in resealable plastic food storage bags.)

Now that your guests have enjoyed several cold appetizers, warm them up with the **Sausage Pinwheels** (page 10) and **Mini Mistletoe Turnovers** (page 15). These two scrumptious treats can be prepared and then frozen, so all you have to do is thaw them properly and serve them as directed in the recipe.

End the festivities with the **Hollyberry Fruit Dip** (page 22). This dip can also be made the night before the party. Serve with an assortment of palate cleansing fresh fruits and shortbread cookies.

simple beginnings

Pepper Cheese Cocktail Puffs

½ package (17¼ ounces) frozen puff pastry, thawed

1 tablespoon Dijon mustard

½ cup (2 ounces) finely shredded Cheddar cheese

1 teaspoon cracked black pepper

1 egg

1 tablespoon water

1. Preheat oven to 400°F. Grease baking sheets.

2. Roll out 1 sheet puff pastry dough on well floured surface to 14×10-inch rectangle. Spread half of dough (from 10-inch side) with mustard. Sprinkle with cheese and pepper. Fold dough over filling; roll gently to seal edges.

3. Cut lengthwise into 3 strips; cut each strip diagonally into 1½-inch pieces. Place on prepared baking sheets. Beat egg and water in small bowl; brush on appetizers.

4. Bake appetizers 12 to 15 minutes or until puffed and deep golden brown. Remove from baking sheet to wire rack to cool.

Makes about 20 appetizers

Prep and Bake Time: 30 minutes

Mini Cocktail Meatballs

1 envelope **LIPTON**® **RECIPE SECRETS**® **Onion, Onion- Mushroom, Beefy Mushroom or Beefy Onion Soup Mix**

1 **pound ground beef**
½ **cup plain dry bread crumbs**
¼ **cup dry red wine or water**
2 **eggs, slightly beaten**

Preheat oven to 375°F.

In medium bowl, combine all ingredients; shape into 1-inch meatballs.

In shallow baking pan, arrange meatballs and bake 18 minutes or until done. Serve, if desired, with assorted mustards or tomato sauce.

Makes about 4 dozen meatballs

make-ahead *recipe*

Sausage Pinwheels

2 **cups biscuit mix**
½ **cup milk**
¼ **cup butter or margarine, melted**

1 **pound BOB EVANS**® **Original Recipe Roll Sausage**

Combine biscuit mix, milk and butter in large bowl until blended. Refrigerate 30 minutes. Divide dough into two portions. Roll out one portion on floured surface to ⅛-inch-thick rectangle, about 10×7 inches. Spread with half the sausage. Roll lengthwise into long roll. Repeat with remaining dough and sausage. Place rolls in freezer until hard enough to cut easily. Preheat oven to 400°F. Cut rolls into thin slices. Place on baking sheets. Bake 15 minutes or until golden brown. Serve hot. Refrigerate leftovers. *Makes 48 appetizers*

NOTE: This recipe may be doubled. Refreeze after slicing. When ready to serve, thaw slices in refrigerator and bake.

Sausage Pinwheels

Sunshine Chicken Drumsticks

½ cup **A.1.**® **Steak Sauce**
¼ **cup ketchup**
¼ **cup apricot preserves**

**12 chicken drumsticks
(about 2½ pounds)**

In small bowl, using wire whisk, blend steak sauce, ketchup and preserves until smooth. Brush chicken with sauce.

Grill chicken over medium heat for 20 minutes or until no longer pink near bone, turning and brushing with remaining sauce. (Do not baste during last 5 minutes of grilling.) Serve hot.   *Makes 12 appetizers*

Holiday Appetizer Puffs

**1 sheet frozen puff
    pastry, thawed (½ of
    17¼-ounce package)
2 tablespoons olive or
    vegetable oil
    Toppings: grated
    Parmesan cheese,**

**sesame seeds, poppy
seeds, dried dill weed,
dried basil leaves,
paprika, drained
capers, pimiento-
stuffed green olive
slices**

Preheat oven to 425°F. Roll pastry on lightly floured surface to 13-inch square. Cut into shapes with cookie cutters (simple-shaped cutters work best). Place on ungreased baking sheets.

Brush cut-outs lightly with oil. Decorate with desired toppings.

Bake 6 to 8 minutes or until golden. Serve warm or at room temperature.   *Makes about 1½ dozen appetizers*

Party Chicken Sandwiches

1½ cups finely chopped
    cooked chicken
1 cup **MIRACLE WHIP®**
    Salad Dressing
1 can (4 ounces) chopped
    green chilies, drained
¾ cup (3 ounces) **KRAFT®**
    Natural Shredded
    Sharp Cheddar
    Cheese

¼ cup finely chopped
    onion
36 party rye or
    pumpernickel bread
    slices

• Combine chicken, salad dressing, chilies, cheese and onions; mix lightly.

• Cover bread with chicken mixture.

• Broil 5 minutes or until lightly browned. Serve hot. Garnish as desired. *Makes 3 dozen sandwiches*

Prep Time: 15 minutes
Broiling Time: 5 minutes

Celebration Brie

1 (12- to 16-ounce) round
    Brie cheese, room
    temperature
1 teaspoon coarsely
    ground black pepper
½ cup **SMUCKER'S®**
    Strawberry Preserves

1 tablespoon balsamic
    vinegar
½ cup chopped **BLUE**
    RIBBON® Calimyrna
    or Mission Figs
Assorted crackers

Sprinkle top of Brie with pepper; press gently into cheese. Mix preserves with vinegar. Stir in figs. Spoon mixture over cheese. Serve with assorted crackers. *Makes 12 servings*

14

Mini Mistletoe Turnovers

1 envelope **LIPTON**® **RECIPE SECRETS**® Onion Soup Mix
2 eggs, beaten
1 package (10 ounces) frozen chopped spinach, cooked and drained
2 cups (16 ounces) ricotta or creamed cottage cheese

1 scant cup (about 3 ounces) shredded mozzarella cheese
3 packages (8 ounces each) refrigerated crescent rolls

Preheat oven to 375°F.

In large bowl, combine onion soup mix, eggs, spinach and cheeses.

Separate crescent rolls according to package directions; cut each triangle in half (to make 2 smaller triangles) and flatten slightly. Place 1 tablespoon cheese mixture on center of each triangle; fold over and seal edges tightly with fork. Place on ungreased baking sheet; bake 15 minutes or until golden brown. *Makes 48 turnovers*

Freezing/Reheating Directions: Tightly wrap turnovers in heavy-duty foil; freeze. To reheat, unwrap and bake as directed for 8 minutes or until heated through.

Cheese Pine Cones

2 cups (8 ounces)
   shredded Swiss
   cheese
½ cup butter or
   margarine, softened
3 tablespoons milk
2 tablespoons dry sherry
   or milk
⅛ teaspoon ground red
   pepper

1 cup finely chopped
   blanched almonds
¾ cup slivered blanched
   almonds
¾ cup sliced almonds
½ cup whole almonds
   Fresh rosemary sprigs
   Assorted crackers

Beat cheese, butter, milk, sherry and red pepper in medium bowl until smooth; stir in chopped almonds.

Divide mixture into 3 equal portions; shape each into tapered ovals to resemble pine cones. Insert slivered, sliced and whole almonds into cones. Cover; refrigerate 2 to 3 hours or until firm.

Arrange Cheese Pine Cones on wooden board or serving plate. Garnish tops with rosemary. Serve with assorted crackers.

Makes 12 to 16 appetizer servings

Cheese Pine Cones

Pesto Brie

2 tablespoons **GREY POUPON**® Dijon Mustard

2 tablespoons prepared pesto sauce

1 (8-ounce) wheel **Brie** cheese

2 tablespoons **PLANTERS**® Walnuts, finely chopped

Chopped tomatoes and fresh basil leaves, for garnish

Assorted **NABISCO**® Crackers or **STELLA D'ORO**® Breadsticks

In small bowl, blend mustard and pesto; set aside. Cut cheese in half horizontally. Place bottom half on greased baking sheet, cut-side up; spread with half the pesto mixture. Replace top of Brie, cut-side down; spread with remaining pesto mixture and sprinkle with nuts.

Bake at 350°F for 3 to 4 minutes or until cheese is slightly softened. Do not overbake. Transfer to serving dish. Garnish with chopped tomatoes and basil leaves. Serve with assorted crackers or breadsticks.

Makes 6 to 8 appetizer servings

Mexicali Appetizer Meatballs

⅔ cup **A.1.**® Steak Sauce

⅔ cup thick and chunky salsa

1½ pounds ground beef

1 egg

½ cup plain dry bread crumbs

In small bowl, blend steak sauce and salsa. In separate small bowl, combine beef, egg, bread crumbs and ⅓ cup sauce mixture; shape into 32 (1¼-inch) meatballs. Arrange meatballs in single layer in shallow baking pan. Bake at 425°F for 12 to 15 minutes or until meatballs are cooked through. Serve hot meatballs with remaining sauce mixture as a dip.

Makes 32 (1¼-inch) meatballs

18

Pesto Brie

Cheesy Christmas Trees

½ cup mayonnaise

1 tablespoon dry ranch-style salad dressing mix

1 cup shredded Cheddar cheese

¼ cup grated Parmesan cheese

12 slices firm white bread

¼ cup red bell pepper strips

¼ cup green bell pepper strips

1. Preheat broiler. Combine mayonnaise and salad dressing mix in medium bowl. Add cheeses; mix well.

2. Cut bread slices into Christmas tree shapes using large cookie cutters. Spread each tree with about 1 tablespoon mayonnaise mixture. Decorate with red and green bell pepper strips. Place on baking sheet.

3. Broil 4 inches from heat 2 to 3 minutes or until bubbling. Serve warm.

Makes about 12 appetizers

Helpful Hints

Mix it up! Cut the bread into stars or bells and decorate with chopped bell pepper for a fun and different holiday feel.

Cheesy Christmas Trees

dips and spreads

Hollyberry Fruit Dip

1 tub (8 ounces) softened cream cheese
½ cup **KARO®** Light Corn Syrup
2 tablespoons sugar

½ cup light sour cream
1 cup cranberries, chopped
1 tablespoon grated orange peel

1. In small bowl with wire whisk or mixer at medium speed, beat cream cheese, corn syrup and sugar until fluffy. Blend in sour cream. Fold in cranberries and orange peel.

2. Chill.

3. Serve with fresh fruit dippers or shortbread cookies.

Makes about 2¼ cups

Prep Time: 10 minutes, plus chilling

Helpful Hints

Serve sliced tart apples, such as Granny Smith, with this deliciously sweet dip.

Louisiana Crab Dip with Crudités

1 package (8 ounces)
  cream cheese,
  softened
½ cup sour cream
3 tablespoons horseradish
2 tablespoons chopped
  fresh parsley
1 tablespoon coarse
  ground mustard
2 teaspoons **TABASCO**®
  brand Pepper Sauce

1 cup lump crabmeat
1 bunch baby carrots
1 bunch celery, cut into
  sticks
1 bunch asparagus
  spears, blanched
2 bunches endive
2 red/green bell peppers,
  cored and cut into
  strips

Blend cream cheese, sour cream, horseradish, parsley, mustard and TABASCO® Sauce in medium bowl until well mixed. Stir in crabmeat.

Arrange carrots, celery, asparagus, endive and peppers on large platter. Serve with dip.   *Makes about 2 cups dip*

Pesto Christmas Tree

1 package (8 ounces)
  PHILADELPHIA®
  Cream Cheese

⅓ cup **DI GIORNO**® Pesto
  Cinnamon stick

CUT cream cheese in half diagonally. Place triangles together to form Christmas tree shape on serving plate.

TOP with pesto. Insert cinnamon stick at base of triangle for "tree trunk." Serve with crackers.   *Makes 12 servings*

TIP: Use red pepper cutouts as "ornaments" to decorate tree.

Prep Time: 5 minutes

24

Pesto Christmas Tree

Pesto Cheese Wreath

Parsley-Basil Pesto*
(page 28)
3 packages (8 ounces
each) cream cheese,
softened
½ cup mayonnaise
¼ cup whipping cream or
half-and-half
1 teaspoon sugar
1 teaspoon onion salt

⅓ cup chopped roasted
red peppers or**
pimiento, drained
Pimiento strips and
Italian flat leaf
parsley leaves
(optional)
Assorted crackers and
cut-up vegetables

One-half cup purchased pesto may be substituted for Parsley-Basil Pesto.

**Look for roasted red peppers packed in cans or jars in the Italian food section of
the supermarket.*

Prepare Parsley-Basil Pesto; set aside. Beat cream cheese and
mayonnaise in medium bowl until smooth; beat in cream, sugar and
onion salt.

Line 5-cup ring mold with plastic wrap. Spoon half of cheese mixture
into prepared mold; spread evenly. Spread Parsley-Basil Pesto evenly
over cheese mixture; top with chopped red peppers. Spoon remaining
cheese mixture over peppers; spread evenly. Cover; refrigerate until
cheese mixture is firm, 8 hours or overnight.

Uncover mold; invert onto serving plate. Carefully remove plastic
wrap. Smooth top and sides of wreath with spatula. Garnish with
pimiento strips and parsley leaves, if desired. Serve with assorted
crackers and vegetables.   *Makes 16 to 24 appetizer servings*

continued on page 28

Pesto Cheese Wreath

Parsley-Basil Pesto

**2 cups fresh parsley
leaves**
**¼ cup pine nuts or
slivered almonds**
**2 tablespoons grated
Parmesan cheese**

2 cloves garlic, peeled
**1 tablespoon dried basil
leaves, crushed**
¼ teaspoon salt
**2 tablespoons olive or
vegetable oil**

Process all ingredients except oil in food processor or blender until
finely chopped. With machine running, add oil gradually, processing
until mixture is smooth.   *Makes about ½ cup*

White Pizza Dip

**1 envelope LIPTON®
RECIPE SECRETS®
Savory Herb with
Garlic Soup Mix**
**1 container (8 ounces)
sour cream**
**1 cup (8 ounces) ricotta
cheese**

**1 cup shredded
mozzarella cheese
(about 4 ounces),
divided**
**¼ cup chopped pepperoni
(about 1 ounce)
(optional)**

1. Preheat oven to 350°F. In 1-quart casserole, combine soup mix,
sour cream, ricotta cheese, ¾ cup mozzarella cheese and pepperoni.
Sprinkle with remaining ¼ cup mozzarella cheese.

2. Bake uncovered 30 minutes or until heated through. Serve with
bread.   *Makes 2 cups dip*

White Pizza Dip

Roasted Eggplant Spread

1 large eggplant
1 can (14½ ounces) diced
   tomatoes, drained
½ cup finely chopped
   green onions
½ cup chopped fresh
   parsley
2 tablespoons red wine
   vinegar

1 tablespoon olive oil
3 cloves garlic, minced
½ teaspoon salt
½ teaspoon dried oregano
   leaves
2 pita breads
   Lemon and lime slices
   (optional)

1. Preheat oven to 375°F.

2. Place eggplant on baking sheet. Bake 1 hour or until tender, turning occasionally. Remove eggplant from oven. Let stand 10 minutes or until cool enough to handle.

3. Cut eggplant lengthwise in half; remove pulp. Place pulp in medium bowl; mash with fork until smooth. Add tomatoes, onions, parsley, vinegar, oil, garlic, salt and oregano; blend well. Cover eggplant mixture; refrigerate 2 hours.

4. Preheat broiler. Split pita breads horizontally in half to form 4 rounds. Stack rounds; cut into sixths to form 24 wedges. Place wedges on baking sheet. Broil 3 minutes or until crisp.

5. Serve eggplant spread with warm pita bread wedges. Garnish with lemon and lime slices, if desired.   *Makes 4 servings*

Roasted Eggplant Spread

New Year's Crystal Ball

10 ounces (2½ cups) shredded Monterey Jack cheese

2 packages (3 ounces each) cream cheese, softened, divided

⅓ cup finely chopped onion

¼ cup mayonnaise

1 teaspoon chili powder

⅓ cup chopped red bell pepper

⅓ cup chopped pitted ripe olives

1 to 2 tablespoons milk

1 large red bell pepper

6 whole pitted ripe olives

Celestial Crackers (page 34)

1. Beat Monterey Jack cheese, 1 package cream cheese, onion, mayonnaise and chili powder in medium bowl until smooth. Mix in chopped red pepper and chopped olives. Shape mixture into ball. Cover with plastic wrap and refrigerate until firm, about 2 hours.

2. Beat remaining package cream cheese in small bowl until fluffy; beat in enough milk to make good spreading consistency. Spread mixture on cheese ball; refrigerate loosely covered until serving time.

3. Cut red pepper into stars with small cutter or sharp knife. Slice olives into crescent moons.

4. Just before serving, decorate cheese ball with stars and moons. Place cheese ball on inverted mug or small plate. Serve with Celestial Crackers.

Makes 12 to 14 servings

continued on page 34

New Year's Crystal Ball

New Year's Crystal Ball, continued

Celestial Crackers

1 cup all-purpose flour	**1 egg white**
½ teaspoon baking powder	**Toppings: Sesame seeds, poppy seeds, garlic salt and dried herbs**
½ teaspoon paprika	**SUPPLIES**
¼ teaspoon salt	**2-inch star- and moon-shaped cookie cutters**
⅓ cup plus 1 tablespoon water, divided	
3 tablespoons vegetable oil	

1. Combine flour, baking powder, paprika and salt in medium bowl. Stir in ⅓ cup water and oil to form smooth dough.

2. Preheat oven to 400°F. Grease baking sheets.

3. Roll dough on floured surface to 14×12-inch rectangle. Cut dough into star and moon shapes using cutters. Place on prepared baking sheets.

4. Combine egg white and 1 tablespoon water; brush on crackers. Sprinkle with toppings.

5. Bake 8 to 10 minutes until edges begin to brown. Remove to wire rack; cool completely.   *Makes 12 to 14 servings*

Eight Layer Fiesta Dip

1 package (1.25 ounces)
    LAWRY'S® Taco
    Spices & Seasonings
1 pound ground beef
¾ cup water
1 can (16 ounces) refried
    beans
½ cup (2 ounces)
    shredded Cheddar
    cheese
1 can (2¼ ounces) sliced
    black olives, drained

1 medium tomato,
    chopped
1 large avocado, peeled
    and coarsely mashed
½ cup dairy sour cream
½ cup salsa
¼ cup thinly sliced green
    onions
    Tortilla chips

In medium skillet, prepare Taco Spices & Seasonings with ground beef and water according to package directions. Add refried beans and cook over low heat 5 minutes. In shallow 1-quart serving bowl, spread beef and bean mixture. Layer remaining ingredients in order given above. Serve immediately with tortilla chips for dipping. *Makes 8 servings*

SERVING SUGGESTION: Fruit juice coolers are ideal for a refreshing accompaniment.

Helpful Hints

Don't let your hard work go unnoticed. Serve this colorful dip in a clear glass serving bowl.

handful of
snacks

Fiesta Chicken Nachos

1 tablespoon olive or
    vegetable oil
1 pound boneless, skinless
    chicken breasts
1 jar (17 ounces) RAGÚ®
    Cheese Creations!®
    Spicy Cheddar &
    Tomato Pasta Sauce

1 bag (9 ounces) tortilla
    chips
2 green and/or red bell
    peppers, diced
1 small onion, chopped
1 large tomato, diced

In 12-inch skillet, heat oil over medium-high heat and cook chicken, stirring occasionally, 8 minutes or until no longer pink. Remove from skillet; cut into strips.

In same skillet, combine chicken and Ragú® Cheese Creations!® Pasta Sauce; heat through.

On serving platter, arrange layer of tortilla chips, then ½ of the sauce mixture, bell peppers, onion and tomato; repeat, ending with tomato. Garnish, if desired, with chopped fresh cilantro and shredded lettuce.

Makes 4 servings

RECIPE TIP: For a spicier dish, add chopped jalapeño peppers or hot pepper sauce to suit your taste.

Sun-Dried Tomato Pizza Snack Mix

2 cups wheat cereal
   squares
2 cups unsweetened
   puffed corn cereal
2 cups puffed rice cereal
2 cups square mini
   cheese crackers
1 cup roasted sunflower
   seeds
3 tablespoons grated
   Parmesan cheese
3 tablespoons butter

2 tablespoons olive oil
2 teaspoons dried Italian
   seasoning
1½ teaspoons garlic powder
¼ cup tomato sauce
1 teaspoon balsamic
   vinegar
⅜ teaspoon sugar
⅛ teaspoon salt
8 to 9 sun-dried tomatoes
   packed in oil, diced

1. Preheat oven to 250°F. Spray 13×9-inch baking pan with nonstick cooking spray.

2. Combine cereal squares, puffed corn, puffed rice, cheese crackers and sunflower seeds in large bowl; set aside.

3. Combine cheese, butter, oil, Italian seasoning and garlic powder in medium bowl. Microwave on HIGH (100%) 1 to 1½ minutes until foamy and herbs release their aromas. Stir in tomato sauce, vinegar, sugar and salt. Pour over cereal mixture; stir well to coat. Place in prepared pan and spread to one layer.

4. Bake 55 to 60 minutes, stirring every 15 minutes. Stir in sun-dried tomatoes 15 minutes before finished baking. Cool, uncovered, in pan on wire rack about 2 hours or until mixture is crisp and tomato pieces have lost their moisture. Store in airtight container or resealable plastic food storage bag.

Makes 7 cups

Sun-Dried Tomato Pizza Snack Mix

Mexicali Crunch

4 cups corn flakes
2 quarts popped corn
3 cups corn or tortilla
    chips
1 cup roasted peanuts
½ cup **MAZOLA**®
    Margarine

½ cup **KARO**® Light or
    Dark Corn Syrup
¼ cup packed brown
    sugar
1 package (1.25 ounces)
    taco seasoning mix

1. Preheat oven to 250°F. In large roasting pan combine corn flakes, popped corn, corn chips and peanuts.

2. In medium saucepan combine margarine, corn syrup, brown sugar and taco seasoning. Bring to boil over medium heat, stirring constantly. Pour over corn flake mixture; toss to coat well.

3. Bake 60 minutes, stirring every 15 minutes. Cool, stirring frequently. Store in tightly covered container. For a Texicali version of this spicy snack, substitute 5 tablespoons of chili seasoning mix for the taco seasoning.   *Makes about 4 quarts*

MICROWAVE DIRECTIONS: In large roasting pan combine corn flakes, popped corn, corn chips and peanuts. In 1-quart microwavable bowl combine margarine, corn syrup, brown sugar and taco seasoning. Microwave on HIGH (100%), 2 to 4 minutes or until mixture boils, stirring once. Pour over corn flake mixture; toss to coat well. Bake as directed.

Prep Time: 20 minutes
Bake Time: 60 minutes, plus cooling

Quick Pimiento Cheese Snacks

2 ounces cream cheese, softened
½ cup (2 ounces) shredded Cheddar cheese
1 jar (2 ounces) diced pimiento, drained

2 tablespoons finely chopped pecans
½ teaspoon hot pepper sauce
24 French bread slices, about ¼ inch thick, or party bread slices

1. Preheat broiler.

2. Combine cream and Cheddar cheeses in small bowl; mix well. Stir in pimiento, pecans and hot pepper sauce.

3. Place bread slices on broiler pan or nonstick baking sheet. Broil, 4 inches from heat, 1 to 2 minutes or until lightly toasted on both sides.

4. Spread cheese mixture evenly onto bread slices. Broil 1 to 2 minutes or until cheese mixture is hot and bubbly. Transfer to serving plate; garnish if desired.   *Makes 24 servings*

Orange-Candied Walnuts

1½ cups sugar
½ cup corn syrup
2 tablespoons butter

4 cups California walnuts
1 teaspoon orange extract

Melt sugar, corn syrup and butter in large, shallow pan over medium-high heat. Add walnuts. Cook and stir about 15 minutes or until sugar mixture begins to caramelize. Stir in extract. Spread walnut mixture evenly onto greased baking sheet, separating walnuts into small clusters. Cool completely.   *Makes 4 cups*

Favorite recipe from **Walnut Marketing Board**

Easy Caramel Popcorn

MAZOLA NO STICK®
Cooking Spray
3 quarts popped popcorn
3 cups unsalted mixed
nuts
1 cup packed brown sugar
½ cup **KARO®** Light or
Dark Corn Syrup

½ cup (1 stick) **MAZOLA®**
Margarine or butter
½ teaspoon salt
½ teaspoon baking soda
½ teaspoon vanilla

1. Spray large shallow roasting pan with cooking spray. Combine popcorn and nuts in pan; place in 250°F oven while preparing glaze.

2. In heavy 2-quart saucepan combine brown sugar, corn syrup, margarine and salt. Stirring constantly, bring to boil over medium heat. Without stirring, boil 5 minutes. Remove from heat; stir in baking soda and vanilla. Pour syrup mixture over warm popcorn and nuts, stirring to coat.

3. Bake in 250°F oven 60 minutes, stirring occasionally. Remove from oven. Cool; break apart. Store in tightly covered container.

Makes about 4 quarts

Prep Time: 10 minutes
Bake Time: 60 minutes, plus cooling

Helpful Hints

Popcorn treats make fun and thoughtful gifts.
Place individual portions of popcorn on cellophane
sheets. Gather up the ends and tie together
with decorative ribbons.

Easy Caramel Popcorn

Praline Pecans & Cranberries

3½ cups pecan halves
¼ cup light corn syrup
¼ cup packed light brown sugar
2 tablespoons butter or margarine

1 teaspoon vanilla
¼ teaspoon baking soda
1½ cups dried cranberries or cherries

1. Preheat oven to 250°F. Grease 13×9-inch baking pan; set aside. Cover large baking sheet with heavy-duty foil; set aside.

2. Spread pecans in single layer in prepared baking pan.

3. Combine corn syrup, sugar and butter in small microwavable bowl. Microwave at HIGH (100%) 1 minute. Stir. Microwave 30 seconds to 1 minute or until boiling rapidly. Stir in vanilla and baking soda until well blended. Drizzle evenly over pecans; stir with wooden spoon until evenly coated.

4. Bake 1 hour, stirring every 20 minutes with wooden spoon. Immediately transfer mixture to prepared baking sheet, spreading pecans evenly over foil with lightly greased spatula.

5. Cool completely. Break pecans apart with wooden spoon. Combine pecans and cranberries in large bowl.

6. Store in airtight container at room temperature up to 2 weeks.

Makes about 5 cups

44

Praline Pecans & Cranberries

Savory Sweet Potato Sticks

3 medium sweet potatoes (about 1½ pounds)
3 cups **KELLOGG'S® RICE KRISPIES®** cereal, crushed to ¾ cup
½ teaspoon garlic salt
¼ teaspoon onion salt
⅛ teaspoon cayenne
½ cup all-purpose flour
2 egg whites
2 tablespoons water
Vegetable cooking spray
Salsa (optional)

1. Wash potatoes and cut lengthwise into ½-inch slices. Cut slices into ½-inch strips. Set aside.

2. In shallow pan or plate, combine Kellogg's Rice Krispies® cereal and spices. Set aside. Place flour in second shallow pan or plate. Set aside. Beat together egg whites and water. Set aside. Coat potatoes with flour, shaking off excess. Dip coated potatoes in egg mixture, then coat with cereal mixture. Place in single layer on foil-lined baking sheet coated with cooking spray.

3. Bake at 400°F about 30 minutes or until lightly browned. Serve hot with salsa, if desired.   *Makes 15 servings*

Prep Time: 25 minutes
Bake Time: 30 minutes

Potpourri Party Mix

½ cup butter, melted
2 teaspoons Worcestershire sauce
½ to 1 teaspoon LAWRY'S® Seasoned Salt
¼ to ½ teaspoon LAWRY'S® Garlic Powder with Parsley

1 quart cubed sourdough bread
1 jar (8½ ounces) dry roasted peanuts
¾ cup diced cheddar cheese
8 bacon strips, cooked and crumbled

In small bowl, combine butter, Worcestershire sauce and seasonings; mix well. On jelly-roll or oblong cake pan, toss bread cubes with seasoned butter. Bake, uncovered, in 350°F oven 20 minutes, stirring occasionally. Cool thoroughly; combine with remaining ingredients.

Makes about 1½ quarts

SERVING SUGGESTION: Serve in attractive serving bowls or napkin-lined baskets.

Spicy Baked Wonton Snacks

12 wonton wrappers
1 tablespoon vegetable oil
¼ teaspoon onion powder

⅛ teaspoon salt
⅛ teaspoon ground red pepper (cayenne)

Cut wonton wrappers lengthwise into thirds. Lay strips in single layer on large baking sheet. Combine oil, onion powder, salt and red pepper in small bowl; brush both sides of strips lightly with oil mixture. Bake in 300°F oven 12 to 13 minutes, or until golden brown. Remove strips to rack to cool.

Makes 3 dozen pieces

Favorite recipe from **Kikkoman International Inc.**

Cranberry-Orange Snack Mix

2 cups oatmeal cereal squares
2 cups corn cereal squares
2 cups mini pretzels
1 cup whole almonds
¼ cup butter
⅓ cup frozen orange juice concentrate, thawed

3 tablespoons packed brown sugar
1 teaspoon ground cinnamon
¾ teaspoon ground ginger
¼ teaspoon ground nutmeg
⅔ cup dried cranberries

1. Preheat oven to 250°F. Spray 13×9-inch baking pan with nonstick cooking spray.

2. Combine cereal squares, pretzels and almonds in large bowl; set aside.

3. Melt butter in medium microwavable bowl on HIGH (100%) 45 to 60 seconds. Stir in orange juice concentrate, brown sugar, cinnamon, ginger and nutmeg until blended. Pour over cereal mixture; stir well to coat. Place in prepared pan and spread to one layer.

4. Bake 50 minutes, stirring every 10 minutes. Stir in cranberries. Let cool in pan on wire rack, leaving uncovered until mixture is crisp. Store in airtight container or resealable plastic food storage bag.

Makes 8 cups

Cranberry-Orange Snack Mix

Ham and Gouda Quesadilla Snacks

1½ cups shredded smoked
    Gouda cheese
    (6 ounces)
1 cup chopped ham
    (4 ounces)
½ cup pitted ripe olives,
    chopped
¼ cup minced red onion

½ cup **GREY POUPON®**
    COUNTRY DIJON®
    Mustard
8 (6- or 7-inch) flour
    tortillas
Sour cream, chopped
    peppers, sliced pitted
    ripe olives and
    cilantro, for garnish

In small bowl, combine cheese, ham, olives and onion. Spread 1 tablespoon mustard on each tortilla; spread about ⅓ cup cheese mixture over half of each tortilla. Fold tortilla in half to cover filling.

In large nonstick skillet, over medium heat, heat filled tortillas for 4 minutes or until cheese melts, turning once. Cut each quesadilla into 3 wedges. Place on serving platter; garnish with sour cream, peppers, olives and cilantro.

Makes 24 appetizers

Party Mix with Cocoa

½ cup (1 stick) margarine
2 tablespoons sugar
2 tablespoons
    HERSHEY®S Cocoa
3 cups bite-size crisp
    wheat squares cereal

3 cups toasted oat cereal
    rings
2 cups miniature pretzels
1 cup salted peanuts
2 cups raisins

Place margarine in 4-quart microwave-safe bowl; microwave at HIGH (100%) 1 to 1½ minutes or until melted. Stir in sugar and cocoa. Add cereals, pretzels and peanuts to margarine mixture; stir until well coated. Microwave at HIGH 3 minutes, stirring every minute. Stir in raisins. Microwave at HIGH 3 minutes, stirring every minute. Cool completely. Store in airtight container at room temperature.

Makes 10 cups mix

Ham and Gouda Quesadilla Snacks

Zesty Party Snack Mix

4 cups oven-toasted corn cereal squares

2 cans (1½ ounces each) FRENCH'S® Potato Sticks

1 cup honey-roasted peanuts

3 tablespoons melted butter or vegetable oil

2 tablespoons FRENCH'S® Worcestershire Sauce

2 tablespoons FRANK'S® REDHOT® Hot Sauce

½ teaspoon seasoned salt

1. Place cereal, potato sticks and peanuts in 3-quart microwavable bowl. Combine melted butter, Worcestershire, Redhot® sauce and seasoned salt in small bowl; mix well. Pour butter mixture over cereal mixture. Toss to coat evenly.

2. Microwave, uncovered, on HIGH 6 minutes, stirring well every 2 minutes. Transfer to paper towels; cool completely.

Makes about 6 cups mix

Tex-Mex Snack Mix: Add 1 teaspoon each chili powder and ground cumin to butter mixture. Substitute 1 cup regular peanuts for honey-roasted nuts. Prepare as directed.

Italian Snack Mix: Add 1½ teaspoons Italian seasoning and ½ teaspoon garlic powder to butter mixture. Substitute ½ cup grated Parmesan cheese and ½ cup sliced almonds for honey-roasted nuts. Prepare as directed.

Indian Snack Mix: Omit seasoned salt. Add 2 teaspoons each sesame seeds and curry powder and ¼ teaspoon garlic salt to butter mixture. Substitute 1 cup cashews for honey-roasted nuts. Prepare as directed.

Prep Time: 10 minutes
Cook Time: 6 minutes

Citrus Candied Nuts

1 egg white	2 teaspoons grated orange peel
1½ cups whole almonds	1 teaspoon grated lemon peel
1½ cups pecan halves	
1 cup powdered sugar	⅛ teaspoon ground nutmeg
2 tablespoons lemon juice	

Preheat oven to 300°F. Generously grease 15½×10½×1-inch jelly-roll pan. Beat egg white in medium bowl with electric mixer on high speed until soft peaks form. Add almonds and pecans; stir until coated. Stir in powdered sugar, lemon juice, orange peel, lemon peel and nutmeg. Turn out onto prepared pan, spreading nuts in single layer.

Bake 30 minutes, stirring after 20 minutes. Turn off oven. Let nuts stand in oven 15 minutes. Remove nuts from pan to sheet of foil. Cool completely. Store up to 2 weeks in airtight container.

Makes about 3 cups

Helpful Hints

Since this snack stores well, it is a great treat to have around the house especially when unexpected guests stop by.

it's salsa time

Venezuelan Salsa

1 mango, peeled, pitted and diced

½ medium papaya, peeled, seeded and diced

½ medium avocado, peeled, pitted and diced

1 carrot, finely chopped

1 small onion, finely chopped

1 rib celery, finely chopped

Juice of 1 lemon

3 cloves garlic, minced

2 tablespoons chopped cilantro

1 jalapeño pepper,* finely chopped

1½ teaspoons ground cumin

½ teaspoon salt

*Jalapeño peppers can sting and irritate the skin; wear rubber gloves when handling peppers and do not touch eyes. Wash hands after handling.

Combine all ingredients in medium bowl. Refrigerate several hours to allow flavors to blend. Serve with baked tortilla chips, carrot and celery sticks or apple wedges. *Makes 2½ cups*

54

Creamy Salsa Dip

1½ cups prepared
    HIDDEN VALLEY®
    Original Ranch® salad
    dressing
2 tomatoes, peeled,
    seeded and chopped
½ cup shredded Monterey
    Jack cheese
¼ cup sliced almonds

¼ cup mild or hot green
    chile peppers, seeded
    and minced
1 green onion, finely
    chopped
Additional sliced
    almonds
Fresh cilantro

In medium bowl, combine all ingredients; mix well. Refrigerate at least
1 hour before serving. Garnish with additional almonds and cilantro.
Serve with taco chips or fresh vegetables. *Makes about 2 cups*

make-ahead *recipe*

Bell Pepper Salsa

1 cup chopped tomatoes
1 yellow or green bell
    pepper, chopped
2 jalapeño peppers,*
    seeded and finely
    chopped
2 tablespoons chopped
    fresh cilantro

2 tablespoons chopped
    onion
2 teaspoons red wine
    vinegar
¼ teaspoon salt

*Jalapeños can sting and irritate the skin; wear rubber gloves when handling peppers and do not touch eyes. Wash hands after handling.

Combine all ingredients in medium bowl. Refrigerate several hours to
let flavors blend. Serve with tortilla chips. *Makes 2 cups*

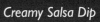
Creamy Salsa Dip

Fresh Salsa

3 medium plum
  tomatoes, seeded
  and chopped
2 tablespoons chopped
  onion
1 small jalapeño pepper,*
  stemmed, seeded
  and minced

1 tablespoon chopped
  cilantro
1 tablespoon lime juice
¼ teaspoon salt
⅛ teaspoon black pepper

*Jalapeño peppers can sting and irritate the skin; wear rubber gloves when handling peppers and do not touch eyes. Wash hands after handling.

Stir together tomatoes, onion, jalapeño pepper, cilantro, lime juice, salt and black pepper in small bowl. Refrigerate until ready to serve.

Makes 1 cup

make-ahead recipe

Avocado Salsa

1 medium avocado,
  peeled and diced
1 cup chopped, seeded
  and peeled cucumber
1 cup chopped onion
1 Anaheim chili,* seeded
  and chopped

½ cup chopped tomato
2 tablespoons chopped
  cilantro
½ teaspoon salt
¼ teaspoon hot pepper
  sauce

*Chili peppers can sting and irritate the skin; wear rubber gloves when handling peppers and do not touch eyes. Wash hands after handling chili peppers.

Combine avocado, cucumber, onion, chili, tomato, cilantro, salt and hot pepper sauce in medium bowl; mix well. Refrigerate, covered, at least 1 hour to allow flavors to blend. Serve as a dip or condiment.

Makes about 4 cups

Pineapple-Mango Salsa

1½ cups DOLE® Fresh
    Pineapple Chunks
1 ripe DOLE® Mango,
    peeled and chopped
½ cup chopped red
    cabbage
⅓ cup finely chopped
    DOLE® Red Onion

¼ cup chopped fresh
    cilantro
2 tablespoons lime juice
1 to 2 serrano or
    jalapeño chiles,
    seeded and minced

• Stir together pineapple, mango, cabbage, red onion, cilantro, lime juice and chiles in medium bowl. Cover and chill for at least 30 minutes to blend flavors. Serve salsa over grilled chicken with grilled vegetables. Garnish with lime wedges, if desired.

• Salsa can also be served as a dip with tortilla chips or spooned over quesadillas or tacos. *Makes 3½ cups*

Fresh Grape Salsa and Chips

¾ cup *each* red and green
    California seedless
    grapes, coarsely
    chopped
½ cup chopped sweet red
    peppers
¼ cup chopped green
    onions
2 tablespoons chopped
    cilantro or basil

1 tablespoon olive oil
1 tablespoon lime juice
2 teaspoons finely
    chopped jalapeño
    pepper
½ teaspoon salt
¼ teaspoon bottled hot
    pepper sauce
Tortilla or bagel chips

Combine all ingredients except chips; mix well. Refrigerate for at least 1 hour to allow flavors to blend. Drain well before serving with chips.
Makes about 1½ cups

Favorite recipe from **California Table Grape Commission**

Black Bean Salsa

1 can (14½ ounces) black beans, rinsed and drained
1 cup frozen corn, thawed
1 large tomato, chopped
¼ cup chopped green onions
2 tablespoons chopped fresh cilantro

2 tablespoons lemon juice
1 tablespoon vegetable oil
1 teaspoon chili powder
¼ teaspoon salt
6 corn tortillas

1. Combine beans, corn, tomato, green onions, cilantro, lemon juice, oil, chili powder and salt in medium bowl; mix well.

2. Preheat oven to 400°F. Cut each tortilla into 8 wedges; place on ungreased baking sheet. Bake 6 to 8 minutes or until edges begin to brown. Serve tortilla wedges warm or at room temperature with salsa. Garnish with lemon wedges and additional fresh cilantro, if desired.

Makes 6 servings

Prep Time: 15 minutes
Chill Time: 30 minutes

Helpful Hints

You can substitute flour tortillas for corn if you prefer, or use a combination of both.

Black Bean Salsa

party
favorites

Mushroom Parmesan Crostini

1 tablespoon olive or
    vegetable oil
1 clove garlic, finely
    chopped
1 cup chopped
    mushrooms
1 loaf Italian or French
    bread (about 12
    inches long), cut into
    12 slices and toasted

¾ cup **RAGÚ® Pizza
    Quick® Sauce**
¼ cup grated **Parmesan
    cheese**
1 tablespoon finely
    chopped fresh basil
    leaves *or* 1 teaspoon
    dried basil leaves

Preheat oven to 375°F. In 8-inch nonstick skillet, heat oil over medium heat and cook garlic 30 seconds. Add mushrooms and cook, stirring occasionally, 2 minutes or until liquid evaporates.

On baking sheet, arrange bread slices. Evenly spread Ragú® Pizza Quick Sauce on bread slices, then top with mushroom mixture, cheese and basil. Bake 15 minutes or until heated through.   *Makes 12 crostini*

RECIPE TIP: Many varieties of mushrooms are available in supermarkets and specialty grocery stores. Shiitake, portobello and cremini mushrooms all have excellent flavor.

East Meets West Cocktail Franks

1 cup prepared sweet
and sour sauce
1 ½ tablespoons rice vinegar
or cider vinegar
1 tablespoon grated fresh
ginger *or* 1 teaspoon
dried ginger
1 tablespoon dark
sesame oil

½ teaspoon chile oil
(optional)
1 package (12 ounces)
**HEBREW
NATIONAL**®
Cocktail Beef Franks
2 tablespoons chopped
cilantro or chives

Combine sweet and sour sauce, vinegar, ginger, sesame oil and chile oil in medium saucepan. Bring to a boil over medium heat. Cook 5 minutes or until thickened. Add cocktail franks; cover and cook until heated through. Transfer to chafing dish; sprinkle with cilantro. Serve with frilled wooden picks.

*Makes 12 appetizer servings
(2 cocktail franks per serving)*

Broccoli-Cheese Quesadillas

1 cup (4 ounces)
shredded Cheddar
cheese
½ cup finely chopped
fresh broccoli

2 tablespoons picante
sauce or salsa
4 (6- to 7-inch) corn or
flour tortillas
1 teaspoon butter, divided

1. Combine cheese, broccoli and picante sauce in small bowl; mix well.

2. Spoon ¼ of the cheese mixture onto 1 side of each tortilla; fold tortilla over filling.

3. Melt ½ teaspoon butter in 10-inch nonstick skillet over medium heat. Add 2 quesadillas; cook about 2 minutes on each side or until tortillas are golden brown and cheese is melted. Repeat with remaining butter and quesadillas. Cool completely. *Makes 4 servings*

East Meets West Cocktail Franks

Holiday Cheese Tree

INGREDIENTS

1½ packages (12 ounces) cream cheese, softened

3 cups (12 ounces) shredded Cheddar Cheese

5 tablespoons finely chopped red bell pepper

5 tablespoons finely chopped onion

4½ teaspoons lemon juice

3 teaspoons Worcestershire sauce

1¼ cups chopped fresh parsley

Yellow bell pepper

Cherry tomatoes, halved

Lemon peel, cut into strips

1. Combine cheeses, chopped bell pepper, onion, lemon juice and Worcestershire sauce in medium bowl; mix until well blended. Place on plate. Shape with hands to form cone shape, about 8 inches tall.

2. Press parsley evenly onto cheese tree.

3. Using small star-shaped cookie cutter, cut star from yellow bell pepper. Place on top of cheese tree. Decorate tree with tomato halves and lemon peel as desired.

4. Serve with assorted crackers and breadsticks.

Makes about 7½ cups (20 to 24 appetizer servings)

Holiday Cheese Tree

Honey Nut Brie

¼ cup coarsely chopped
    pecans
¼ cup honey
  1 tablespoon brandy
    (optional)

1 wheel (14 ounces) Brie
   cheese (about 5-inch
   diameter)

Combine pecans, honey and brandy, if desired, in small bowl. Place cheese on large round ovenproof platter or 9-inch pie plate. Bake in preheated 500°F oven 4 to 5 minutes or until cheese softens. Drizzle honey mixture over top of cheese. Bake 2 to 3 minutes longer or until topping is thoroughly heated. *Do not melt cheese.*

Makes 16 to 20 servings

Coconut-Orange Shrimp

2½ cups flaked coconut,
    divided
  1 medium ripe banana
¼ cup FRANK'S®
    REDHOT® Hot Sauce
¼ cup orange juice

1 tablespoon olive oil
1 tablespoon grated
   orange peel
1 pound raw large
   shrimp, shelled and
   deveined

1. Combine ½ cup coconut, banana, Redhot® sauce, juice, oil and orange peel in blender or food processor; process until puréed.

2. Pour into resealable plastic food storage bag. Add shrimp; toss to coat. Seal bag. Refrigerate 1 hour.

3. Preheat oven to 450°F. Line baking pan with foil; grease foil. Sprinkle remaining coconut onto sheet of waxed paper. Dip shrimp into coconut, pressing firmly to coat. (Do not shake off excess marinade from shrimp.) Place shrimp on prepared baking pan. Bake 6 to 8 minutes or until shrimp are opaque.

Makes 6 servings

Prep Time: 30 minutes
Cook Time: 6 minutes

68

Coconut-Orange Shrimp

Savory Zucchini Stix

Olive oil-flavored nonstick cooking spray
2 small zucchini (about 4 ounces each)
3 tablespoons seasoned dry bread crumbs
2 tablespoons grated Parmesan cheese
1 egg white
1 teaspoon reduced-fat (2%) milk
1/3 cup spaghetti sauce, heated

1. Preheat oven to 400°F. Spray baking sheet with cooking spray; set aside.

2. Cut zucchini lengthwise into quarters; set aside.

3. Combine bread crumbs and Parmesan cheese in shallow dish. Combine egg white and milk in another shallow dish; beat with fork until well blended.

4. Dip each zucchini wedge first into crumb mixture, then into egg white mixture, letting excess drip back into dish. Roll in crumb mixture to coat again.

5. Place zucchini sticks on prepared baking sheet; coat well with cooking spray.

6. Bake 15 to 18 minutes or until golden brown. Serve with spaghetti sauce.

Makes 4 servings

Helpful Hints

If you like your dipping sauce with a little zing, stir in a few drops of hot pepper sauce.

Holiday Star

TOPPING

¾ cup sour cream
½ cup mayonnaise
2 tablespoons heavy
  cream
1 teaspoon balsamic
  vinegar
¼ cup chopped fresh
  cilantro

¼ cup chopped fresh basil
¼ cup chopped roasted
  red peppers, drained
  and patted dry
½ teaspoon garlic powder
¼ teaspoon salt
  Black pepper to taste

STAR

2 cans (8 ounces each)
  refrigerated crescent
  roll dough

GARNISHES

Red bell pepper,
  chopped
Green onion, chopped

Black olive slices
(optional)

1. Preheat oven to 375°F.

2. Combine sour cream, mayonnaise, heavy cream and balsamic vinegar in medium bowl. Stir in cilantro, basil and roasted red pepper. Add garlic powder, salt and black pepper; mix well. Cover and refrigerate at least 1 hour to let flavors blend or until ready to spread.

3. Place 3-inch round cookie cutter or similar size custard cup in center of 14-inch pizza pan; set aside. Remove dough from first can and unroll on cookie sheet. Seal perforations by pressing down slightly with fingers. Cut 24 circles with 1½-inch cookie cutter. Remove excess dough from cut circles; set aside. Repeat with second can.

continued on page 72

Holiday Star, continued

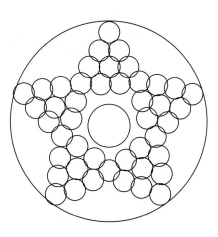

4. Place five dough circles evenly spaced around the outside edge of pizza pan (these will be the star points). From each star point, make a triangle pattern with rows of slightly overlapping dough circles working toward the cookie cutter in center of pan (see diagram). Roll excess dough into a ball; flatten with hands. Cut more circles as needed to completely fill in star.

5. Remove cookie cutter in center of star. Bake 12 to 16 minutes or until star is light golden brown. Cool completely, in pan on wire rack, about 30 minutes.

6. Spread topping over star. Garnish with red bell pepper, green onion and black olives, if desired. Place decorative candle in center of star. Serve immediately. *Makes about 16 servings*

Helpful Hints

Instead of placing candle in center of star, hollow out a red or green bell pepper and fill it with any remaining dip. Place fresh vegetables, such as broccoli florets or bell pepper strips, around the star.

Holiday Star

Rumaki

16 slices bacon
1 pound chicken livers, cut into quarters
1 can (8 ounces) sliced water chestnuts, drained

⅓ cup soy sauce
2 tablespoons packed brown sugar
1 tablespoon Dijon mustard

Cut bacon slices in half crosswise. Wrap ½ slice bacon around piece of chicken liver and water chestnut slice. Secure with wooden pick. (Reserve any remaining water chestnut slices for another use.) Arrange on broiler pan. Combine soy sauce, brown sugar and mustard in small bowl. Brush over bacon rolls. Broil, 6 inches from heat, 15 to 20 minutes or until bacon is crisp and chicken livers are done, turning and brushing with soy sauce mixture occasionally.

Makes about 32 appetizers

Favorite recipe from **National Pork Producers Council**

Fiesta Quesadillas with Fruit Salsa

1 can (11 ounces) DOLE® Mandarin Oranges, drained and finely chopped
1 tablespoon chopped fresh cilantro or fresh parsley
1 tablespoon lime juice
4 (8-inch) whole wheat or flour tortillas
¾ cup shredded low fat Monterey Jack, mozzarella or Cheddar cheese

⅔ cup finely chopped DOLE® Pitted Dates or Chopped Dates or finely chopped Pitted Prunes
⅓ cup crumbled feta cheese
2 tablespoons chopped green onion

- Combine mandarin oranges, cilantro and lime juice in small bowl for salsa; set aside.

- Place two tortillas on large baking sheet. Sprinkle half of shredded cheese, dates, feta and green onion over each tortilla to within ½ inch of edge.

- Brush outer ½-inch edge of each tortilla with water. Top with remaining tortillas; press down edges gently to seal.

- Bake at 375°F 5 to 8 minutes or until hot. Cut each quesadilla into 6 wedges.

- Drain salsa just before serving, if desired; serve over warm quesadillas.

Makes 6 servings

Prep Time: 15 minutes
Bake Time: 8 minutes

Seafood Cocktails with Watercress Sauce

2 cups loosely packed stemmed watercress	**¼ cup mayonnaise**
1 cup loosely packed stemmed parsley	**⅛ teaspoon pepper**
1 medium clove garlic, finely chopped	**2 pounds cooked and chilled assorted seafood such as: butterflied shrimp, scallops, crab claws and legs, lobster meat or clams**
1 envelope LIPTON® RECIPE SECRETS® Golden Onion Soup Mix	
½ pint (8 ounces) sour cream	

In food processor or blender, combine watercress, parsley and garlic until blended. Add golden onion soup mix, sour cream, mayonnaise and pepper; process until smooth. Refrigerate at least 2 hours. Serve with assorted seafood. Garnish as desired.   *Makes 8 appetizer servings*

75

Holiday Shrimp Dip

4½ teaspoons unflavored gelatin
¼ cup cold water
1 can (10¾ ounces) condensed tomato soup
1 package (3 ounces) cream cheese
1 cup mayonnaise
1 bag (6 ounces) frozen small shrimp, thawed

¾ cup finely chopped celery
2 tablespoons grated onion
¼ teaspoon salt
White pepper to taste
Bell peppers for garnish (optional)

1. Dissolve gelatin in cold water in small bowl; set aside. Grease four 1-cup holiday mold pans or one 5-cup holiday mold pan; set aside.

2. Heat soup in medium saucepan over medium heat until hot. Add cream cheese; blend well. Add remaining ingredients. Pour into prepared mold; refrigerate 30 minutes. Cover with foil and refrigerate overnight.

3. Decorate with bell peppers cut into holly leaves, if desired. Serve with assorted crackers.   *Makes 12 servings*

Helpful Hints

This dip is great for any occasion and can be made in any shape mold you desire.

Holiday Shrimp Dip

beverage bar

Mulled Apple Cider

2 quarts bottled apple
  cider or juice
  (not unfiltered)
¼ cup packed brown sugar
1 square (8 inches)
  double-thickness
  cheesecloth

8 allspice berries
4 cinnamon sticks,
  broken into halves
12 whole cloves
1 large orange
  Additional cinnamon
  sticks (optional)

SLOW COOKER DIRECTIONS

Combine apple cider and brown sugar in slow cooker. Rinse cheesecloth; squeeze out water. Wrap allspice berries and cinnamon stick halves in cheesecloth; tie securely with cotton string or strip of cheesecloth. Stick cloves randomly into orange; cut orange into quarters. Place spice bag and orange quarters in cider mixture. Cover and cook on HIGH 2½ to 3 hours. Once cooked, cider may be turned to LOW and kept warm up to 3 additional hours. Discard spice bag and orange before serving; ladle cider into mugs. Garnish with additional cinnamon sticks, if desired.   *Makes 10 servings*

Champagne Punch

1 orange
1 lemon
¼ cup cranberry-flavored
    liqueur or cognac
¼ cup orange-flavored
    liqueur or triple sec

1 bottle (750 ml) pink or
    regular champagne
    or sparkling white
    wine, well chilled
Fresh cranberries
    (optional)
Citrus strips for garnish

Remove colored peel, not white pith, from orange and lemon in long thin strips with citrus peeler. Refrigerate orange and lemon for another use. Combine peels and cranberry- and orange-flavored liqueurs in glass pitcher. Cover and refrigerate 2 to 6 hours.

Just before serving, tilt pitcher to one side and slowly pour in champagne. Leave peels in pitcher for added flavor. Place cranberry in bottom of each champagne glass, if desired. Pour into glasses. Garnish with citrus strips tied in knots, if desired. *Makes 4 cups (6 to 8 servings)*

Passion Potion

1½ cups pink grapefruit
    juice, chilled
3 tablespoons honey

Ice cubes
¼ cup rum or vodka*

*If desired, omit rum or vodka and top each glass with ¼ cup club soda.

Combine grapefruit juice and honey in pitcher; stir until honey is dissolved. Fill two 12-ounce glasses with ice. Pour 2 tablespoons rum over ice in each glass and add grapefruit juice mixture.

Makes 2 cups

Favorite recipe from **National Honey Board**

Champagne Punch

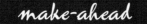

Raspberry Eggnog

½ cup sugar
2 tablespoons cornstarch
4 cups skim milk, divided
2 eggs, beaten
1 package (12 ounces)
    frozen raspberries,
    thawed

1 teaspoon vanilla
6 to 9 drops red food
    coloring
Ground nutmeg

1. Combine sugar and cornstarch in large saucepan; stir in 2 cups milk. Bring to a boil over low heat, stirring constantly. Continue boiling 1 minute or until thickened, stirring constantly. Whisk small amount of hot milk mixture into eggs in small bowl. Whisk egg mixture back into hot milk mixture in saucepan. Cook over low heat 1 minute. Strain; cool.

2. Place raspberries in food processor or blender; process until smooth. Strain; discard seeds. Stir raspberry purée into milk mixture; stir in remaining 2 cups milk and vanilla. Add red food coloring, one drop at a time, until eggnog is desired shade. Cover; refrigerate until cold or ready to serve. Sprinkle each serving with nutmeg. Garnish with mint sprigs and raspberries, if desired.

Makes 12 (½-cup) servings

Viennese Coffee

1 cup heavy cream, divided

1 teaspoon powdered sugar

1 bar (3 ounces) bittersweet or semisweet chocolate

3 cups strong freshly brewed hot coffee

1/4 cup crème de cacao or Irish cream (optional)

Chill bowl, beaters and cream before whipping. Place 2/3 cup cream and sugar into chilled bowl. Beat with electric mixer at high speed until soft peaks form.

Cover and refrigerate up to 8 hours. If mixture has separated slightly after refrigeration, whisk lightly with a wire whisk before using.

To make chocolate shavings for garnish, place waxed paper under chocolate. Holding chocolate in one hand, make short, quick strokes across chocolate with vegetable peeler; set aside. Break remaining chocolate into pieces.

Place remaining 1/3 cup cream in heavy small saucepan. Bring to a simmer over medium-low heat. Add chocolate pieces; cover and remove from heat. Let stand 5 minutes or until chocolate is melted; stir until smooth.

Add hot coffee to chocolate mixture. Heat on low heat just until bubbles form around the edge of pan and coffee is heated through, stirring frequently. Remove from heat; stir in crème de cacao.

Pour into 4 warmed mugs. Top with whipped cream. Garnish with chocolate shavings. *Makes about 4 (3½-cup) servings*

"A French" Banana Smoothie

2 (.53-ounce) envelopes
   SWISS MISS® Fat
   Free French Vanilla
   Cocoa Mix
½ cup fat free milk
½ ripe banana

1 tablespoon wheat germ
   (optional)
1 tablespoon honey
   (optional)
2 cups ice cubes

1. In blender, combine *all* ingredients.

2. Blend until thick and smooth.   *Makes 2 (7-ounce) servings*

make-ahead	recipe

Hot Buttered Cider

⅓ cup packed brown sugar
¼ cup butter or
   margarine, softened
¼ cup honey
¼ teaspoon ground
   cinnamon

¼ teaspoon ground
   nutmeg
Apple cider or juice

1. Beat sugar, butter, honey, cinnamon and nutmeg until well blended and fluffy. Place butter mixture in tightly covered container. Refrigerate up to 2 weeks. Bring butter mixture to room temperature before using.

2. To serve, heat apple cider in large saucepan over medium heat until hot. Fill individual mugs with hot apple cider; stir in 1 tablespoon batter per 1 cup apple cider.   *Makes 12 servings*

Prep and Cook Time: 15 minutes

84

Hot Buttered Cider

Sparkling White Sangria

1 cup **KARO®** Light Corn Syrup
1 orange, sliced
1 lemon, sliced
1 lime, sliced
½ cup orange-flavored liqueur

1 bottle (750 mL) dry white wine
2 tablespoons lemon juice
1 bottle (12 ounces) club soda or seltzer, chilled
Additional fresh fruit (optional)

1. In large pitcher combine corn syrup, orange, lemon and lime slices and liqueur. Let stand 20 to 30 minutes, stirring occasionally.

2. Stir in wine and lemon juice. Refrigerate.

3. Just before serving, add soda and ice cubes. If desired, garnish with additional fruit. *Makes about 6 (8-ounce) servings*

Prep Time: 15 minutes, plus standing and chilling

Christmas Carol Punch

2 medium red apples
2 quarts clear apple cider
½ cup **SUN-MAID®** Raisins
8 cinnamon sticks

2 teaspoons whole cloves
¼ cup lemon juice
Lemon slices
Orange slices

Core apples; slice into ½-inch rings. In Dutch oven, combine cider, apple rings, raisins, cinnamon and cloves. Bring to a boil over high heat; reduce heat to low and simmer 5 to 8 minutes or until apples are just tender. Remove cloves; add lemon juice and lemon and orange slices. Pour into punch bowl. Ladle into large mugs, including an apple ring, some raisins and citrus slices in each serving. Serve with spoons.

Makes about 2 quarts

Sparkling White Sangria

Mocha Nog

1 quart eggnog
1 tablespoon instant
  French vanilla or
  regular coffee
  granules

¼ cup coffee-flavored
  liqueur

1. Heat eggnog and coffee granules in large saucepan over medium heat until mixture is hot and coffee granules are dissolved; *do not boil.* Remove from heat; stir in coffee liqueur.

2. Pour eggnog into individual mugs.   *Makes 8 servings*

Prep and Cook Time: 10 minutes

Coconut Snowball Cocoa

1 pint vanilla ice cream
1 cup flaked coconut
½ cup unsweetened cocoa
1 quart milk
½ cup dark rum (optional)
¾ to 1 cup cream of
  coconut

1 teaspoon coconut
  extract
½ cup chocolate-flavored
  ice cream sauce
  (optional)
8 maraschino cherries
  (optional)

Scoop ice cream into 8 small balls; immediately roll in coconut. Place on waxed paper-lined baking sheet; freeze until ready to use.

Whisk cocoa into milk in large saucepan. Stir in rum, if desired, cream of coconut and coconut extract. Bring to a simmer over medium-high heat. Pour into 8 large heatproof mugs.

Float ice cream balls in cocoa. If desired, drizzle each ice cream ball with chocolate sauce and top with cherry.   *Makes 8 servings*

Mocha Nog

Pineberry Smoothie

1 ripe DOLE® Banana,
    quartered
1 cup DOLE® Pineapple
    Juice
½ cup nonfat vanilla or
    plain yogurt

½ cup fresh or frozen
    strawberries,
    raspberries or
    blueberries

Combine all ingredients in blender or food processor container. Blend until thick and smooth. Serve immediately. *Makes 2 servings*

Prep Time: 5 minutes

make-ahead *recipe*

Spiced Apple Tea

2 cups unsweetened
    apple juice
6 whole cloves
1 cinnamon stick

3 cups water
3 bags cinnamon herbal
    tea

Combine juice, cloves and cinnamon stick in medium saucepan. Bring to a boil over high heat. Reduce heat to low; simmer 10 minutes. Meanwhile, place water in another medium saucepan. Bring to a boil over high heat. Remove from heat; drop in tea bags and allow to steep for 6 minutes. Remove and discard tea bags.

Strain juice mixture; discard spices. Stir juice mixture into tea. Serve warm with additional cinnamon sticks, if desired, or refrigerate and serve cold over ice. (Tea may be made ahead and reheated.)

Makes 4 servings

acknowledgments

The publisher would like to thank the companies and organizations listed below for the use of their recipes and photographs in this publication.

A.1.® Steak Sauce

Bob Evans®

California Table Grape Commission

Colorado Potato Administrative Committee

ConAgra Grocery Products Company

Dole Food Company, Inc.

Grey Poupon® Mustard

Hebrew National®

Hershey Foods Corporation

Hormel Foods Corporation

Kellogg Company

Kikkoman International Inc.

Kraft Foods, Inc.

Lawry's® Foods, Inc.

Lipton®

McIlhenny Company (TABASCO® brand Pepper Sauce)

National Honey Board

National Pork Producers Council

Reckitt & Colman Inc.

Sun•Maid® Growers of California

The J.M. Smucker Company

Walnut Marketing Board

index